HEARING THE VOICE OF GOD,

The Foundation Of The Church

Cassandra Broadnax

HEARING THE VOICE OF GOD

The Foundation Of The Church

By Cassandra Broadnax

Hearing The Voice Of God

The Foundation Of The Church

Table of Contents

<u>Chapter</u>

INTRODUCTION

I was born and raised a Baptist. I accepted Jesus Christ as my Lord and Savior when I was seven years old. In this Baptist church they believed in much teaching of the word of God. And this is good.

In 1975, when I was twenty one years old, I got married. My husband had not given his life to the Lord. His mother's church was nearer where we lived, and I had met so many friends in the area that I decided to move my membership to her church.

Even though I knew that part of the name of the church was Disciples of Christ, I did not realize that they were not Baptist, but Disciples Of Christ. Everything seemed the same to me. And I felt that if my husband ever joined a church, it would be his mother's church, and not the one that I grew up in. And he did, seven years later, just after my second child, a daughter was born.

The beginning of 1985 God began to give me a plan for a business. He would keep me up all night, talking to me as I wrote, while my husband worked third shift. After I had finished writing the plan on paper, He then said to me, Now, go do it.

I did, and He guided me every step of the way. I ran a bridal business, a full service florist, and a catering business all in one.

This lasted for ten years. In the spring of 1995, another florist in the area asked me if I wanted to purchase his business; he was ready to retire. I told him I would buy it; and set out to get the money. I convinced my husband that I could do it, and he agreed to go with me to the bank to get a loan. But by the time the loan officer called to tell me that the loan had been approved, "something" had spoken to me, and told me not to go through with the deal. So I refused the loan, and turned down the offer for the business. Every one thought that I was crazy, because it was such a good deal. The "something" was the Lord, I know that now.

In June of the same year, my father decided that he wanted all of his five daughters and their families (for we all had children and were married, except one), to travel with him and my mother to College Park, GA. To visit my brother who lived there. So we made a little caravan, and drove to Georgia. My mother's mother, my grandmother went with us.

We were in-between pastors at our church. The Sunday before we left, the interim pastor at our church preached "How To Get Out Of A Rut." I needed to hear the sermon, but there was something missing in the sermon. After the sermon, one of the choir members sang a song that touched our hearts. So much that I began to weep, holding my head down to hide my tears.

On my right, I could hear two of the younger women praising the Lord aloud. One was saying, Hallelujah! The other was saying, Thank You Jesus!

I said to the Lord, within myself, Lord, I am tired of hiding my tears this way, I want to praise you, just like those two young women. But nothing happened, at least not then. When we got home from service, my husband said to me, Something happened when she sang that song, didn't it? I answered, You felt it too?

My mother had been to Bible Study the week before. While there she had gone into a trance, and God had spoken to her. Being in that Baptist church, the others attending the Bible Study thought that she was sick, and wanted to get her to the hospital. But they called us first, and we took her home. We knew that something was amidst, and once we saw her we knew that she didn't need to go to a doctor nor to the hospital.

The family left on Friday afternoon going to Georgia, and this is when "something" happened. That Saturday morning my brother cooked breakfast for us all. Afterwards he was about to take the men to some yard sales. Daddy loved to go to yard sales. But the women were going shopping; or you could say, looking, as none of us had any money. Everyone was going but my mother. There was something still amidst about her. It was as if she was still in another world.

As we were about to leave the house, my mother came to the top of the stairs, and told us to come back into the house, to pray. I thought, Oh, no! Here we go. But "something" said to me, Can't you wait about fifteen minutes? I thought, Yes. And as soon as I said yes, a peace came over me.

We all went into the living room. There were twenty one of us, including the children. We all gathered in a circle, and held hands. Then my grand mother began to pray, next my father prayed, and then my mother prayed. It was while my mother was praying that something happened to me. I don't know about the others, but I do know that something happened to me.

I threw up both of my hands and began to shout with a very loud voice, saying, Thank You Jesus, Thank You Jesus! Tears began to run down my face. Something had changed in my heart, and I have never been the same.

At that moment a hunger to really know God came over me. I wanted to understand what had happened to me, but I knew no one in the room could explain it to me. Instead of fifteen minutes, we stayed in that room for three hours, reading the Bible, praising God, and talking. It was so good! I had never experienced anything like it before, and I didn't want to leave, I wanted more.

The next day we attended the church of my brother's girlfriend. It was Youth Sunday, and they had a guest speaker. The speaker was a young woman; a member of the church, who had been away to college. She took her text from Romans 12:1, 2. Her subject was "The Importance of Renewing Your Mind In The Word Of God." Not knowing it then, God had set my family up to hear this message. After the experience on the day before, this was just what we needed. It was the next step.

It was not until the trip home that I found out what had happened to me. Several months before my youngest sister had been trying to get me to read a book. But I never had time, because of my business. My father had taken the book to Georgia to read, and completed it. He returned it to my sister, and she gave it to me just before we pulled off to return home. And I began to read it. The name of the book was "Good Morning Holy Spirit" by Benny Hinn. That is when I found out that I had received the Baptism of the Holy Ghost Saturday morning at my brother's house.

I was so excited, but still I did not know what the Holy Ghost was. They had taught a lot of things in the Baptist Church, but they had not taught about the Holy Ghost. The only time I heard the name Holy Ghost was when someone was baptized, and the pastor would say, I now baptize you in the name of the Father, in the name of the Son, and in the name of the Holy Ghost.

After reading this book I had a hunger to really get to know God's word. In reading the book, I learned that I could talk to God, and He would answer me. That is when I learned who the "something" is. It was God, talking to me all along. I remember when I was a very young girl, I would go alone into the back yard, and talk with God. I would call Him my boyfriend. He always comforted me when I was down, and depressed about something.

The trip to Georgia was in July 1995. By September the same year, I no longer had the desire to run the business. All that I wanted to do was to read my Bible. I had gone out and purchased a special King James Version of the Bible: what they call a Study Bible (The Hebrew – Greek Key Word Study Bible), which really helped me to understand what I was reading.

I told my husband about my desire, and he said, If you want to close the business and come home, You come home honey!

(To Be Continued)

CHAPTER 1

Calling Upon The Name Of The Lord

The Christian faith is different from other beliefs; in that the God we serve and worship has a Son whose name is Jesus Christ, and He also has a Holy Spirit. Although they are three, yet they are one in the same.

The God we serve is alive, therefore Christians have an advantage over other beliefs; we can talk to our God, and we can also hear Him talk to us.

It delights our God that we recognize Him as God, that we would come to Him, and spend time with Him. It delights Him even more when we call upon His name.

Jeremiah 33:2, 3

Thus saith the Lord the maker thereof, the Lord that formed it, to establish it: the Lord is His name;

Call upon me, and I will answer thee, and show thee great and mighty things, which thou knowest not.

I want to reveal to you His delight, in a way in which you may really understand. Remember when you went to visit an elderly man or woman who lived alone? Remember how delighted they were because you came to visit them? Remember how they reacted when you asked questions concerning how to do something or make something? Or you may have asked them to tell you about the greatest joy of their life. And as they talked, you felt that you were in the place that they were describing, standing afar watching the whole scene? Their eyes twinkled as they talked with you.

God has this same delight when we take the time to spend with Him, and when we ask questions. He wants to talk with us face to face.

Exodus 33:11

And the Lord spake unto Moses face to face, as a man speaketh unto his friend. And he turned again into the camp: but his servant Joshua, the son of Nun, a young man, departed not out of the tabernacle.

Moses had been talking with God, and Joshua had been with Moses, listening. But when Moses turned again into the camp, Joshua stayed a while longer to talk with God.

There is an offering we will study about in the next book; which is the very fact that one would stop to spend time with the Lord, and talk with Him.

Most of us will not even recognize that God is there until we are in trouble. That too, is ok, He will still respond, but only if we don't come with murmuring and complaining. He hates when we murmur and complain and He tends to ignore you.

Usually when one calls upon His name, they will ask God a question; this is an offering, a sacrifice. Most people have so much pride that they will not ask. Or they believe they don't have to ask, because God knows. The Bible says, You have not, because you ask not. Which means that you must open your mouth and speak.

We will talk about three different types of questions that we ask when we call upon the name of the Lord, in which God will respond to:

1. Asking God to heal and/or deliver you.
2. Asking God to forgive you of your sin.
3. Asking God to heal and/or deliver someone else.

We will look at the first: Asking God to heal and/or deliver you.

Joel 2:32

And it shall come to pass that whosoever shall call on the name of the Lord shall be delivered: for in mount Zion and in Jerusalem shall be deliverance, as the Lord hath said, and in the remnant whom the Lord shall call.
(This gives anyone the right to call upon the name of God, whether saved or not.)

Examples from the Bible of calling upon the Lord:

Exodus 2:23-25

And it came to pass in the process of time, that the king of Egypt died: and the children of Israel sighed by reason of the bondage, and they cried, and their cry came up unto God by reason of the bondage.

And God heard their groaning, and God remembered His covenant with Abraham, with Isaac, and with Jacob.

And God looked upon the children of Israel, and God had respect unto them.

The man Naaman was a Syrian, a man who worshiped other gods. But he called upon the name of God when he went to Elisha. Although God tested his faith, when Naaman obeyed, he was healed of leprosy.

II Kings 5:9, 10

So Naaman came with his horses and with his chariot, and stood at the door of the house of Elisha.

And Elisha sent a messenger unto him saying, Go and wash in the Jordan seven times, and thy flesh shall come again to thee, and thou shalt be clean.

This next man was a Jew. He made no confession of sin, he simply asked Jesus to heal him. It was after the man was healed that Jesus instructed him to go offer a second sacrifice. But the man went not.

Luke 5:12, 13

And it came to pass, when He was in a certain city, behold a man full of leprosy; who seeing Jesus fell on his face, and besought Him, saying, Lord, if thou wilt, thou canst make me clean.

And He put forth His hand, and touched him, saying, I will: be thou clean. And immediately the leprosy departed from him.

Next we will take a look at the second type of offering: Asking the Lord to forgive you of your sin.

Leviticus 14:1-5

And the Lord spake unto Moses, saying,

This shall be the law of the leper in the day of his cleansing: He shall be brought unto the priest:

And the priest shall go forth out of the camp; and the priest shall look, and, behold, if the plague of leprosy be healed in the leper;

Then shall the priest command to take for him that is to be cleansed two birds alive and clean, and cedar wood, and scarlet, and hyssop:

And the priest shall command that one of the birds be killed in an earthen vessel over running water.

The fact that the leper went to the priest is a sacrifice.

The bird that was killed represents Jesus sacrificing His life for our sins. The dead bird being washed under running water represents the fact that He was without sin. The live bird represents His resurrection. The cedar wood, scarlet and hyssop dipped in the blood of the dead bird represent your cleansing. Jesus made this sacrifice that we might be healed, delivered.

In Psalm 51 we will see the fact that when David called upon the name of the Lord, that he confessed his sin, and that he asked God to cleanse him.

Psalm 51:1-7

Have mercy upon me, O God, according to thy loving kindness: according unto the multitude of thy tender mercies blot out my transgressions.

Wash me thoroughly from mine iniquity, and cleanse me from my sin.

For I acknowledge my transgressions: and my sin is ever before me.

Against thee, thee only, have I sinned, and done this evil in thy sight: that thou mightest be justified when thou speakest, and be clear when thou judgest.

Behold, I was shapen in iniquity; and in sin did my mother conceive me.

Behold, thou desirest truth in the inward parts: and in the hidden part thou shalt make me to know wisdom.

Purge me with hyssop, and I shall be clean: wash me, and I shall be whiter than snow.

When the children of Israel sinned against God by murmuring and complaining, God sent fiery serpents to bite them. Many got sick and died. After they realized what they had done, they went to Moses and repented. Moses interceded for them, and God tested them that their hearts might be exposed.

Not every one had been bitten, only those who had murmured and complained. Of these, only those who humbled themselves before God by coming before the pole were healed. Those who had been bitten and refused to humble themselves before God and the congregation, died from the bite of the serpent. When those who obeyed came before the pole, it was as if they were confessing their sin, and they were forgiven.

Numbers 21:8

And the Lord said unto Moses, Make thee a fiery serpent, and set it upon a pole; and it shall come to pass, that every one that is bitten, when he looketh upon it, shall live.

Next we look at Isaiah, who had heard the voice of God but had not seen the heart of God, and His holiness. When Isaiah saw the holiness of God, he realized his own uncleanness. We will see Isaiah confess his sin, and the cleansing of his sin.

Isaiah 6:5-7

Then said I, Woe is me! For I am undone; because I am a man of unclean lips, and I dwell in the midst of a people of unclean lips: for mine eyes have seen the King, the Lord of hosts.

Then flew one of the seraphims unto me, having a live coal in his hand, which he had taken with the tongs from off the altar.

And he laid it upon my mouth, and said, Lo, this hath touched thy lips; and thine iniquity is taken away, and thy sin purged.

And now we look at the ten lepers in Luke 17. You will see them call upon the name of the Lord, and confess their sin. In asking for mercy they were asking the Lord to forgive them of their sin. You will also see them receive healing.

Luke 17:12-14

And as He entered into a certain village, there met Him ten men that were lepers, which stood afar off:

And they lifted up their voices, and said, Jesus, Master, have mercy on us.

And when He saw them, He said unto them, Go show yourselves unto the priests. And it came to pass, that, as they went, they were cleansed.

The third offering is when one calls upon the name of the Lord to intercede for another to be delivered and/or healed. It could be one's child, or one's friend, or a relative.

This first man, the Bible says is a ruler in the synagogue (Mark 5:22). This man fell down at his feet and worshiped Jesus, asking Him to heal his daughter. He humbled himself and called upon the name of the Lord. Because of his faith, his daughter was healed.

Matthew 9:18

While He spake these things unto them, behold, there came a certain ruler, and worshiped Him, saying, My daughter is even now dead: but come and lay thy hand upon her, and she shall live.

In the next scripture, two sisters calling upon the name of the Lord to come heal their brother. It took a little time but the brother was not only healed, but was raised from the dead.

John 11:1-4

Now a certain man was sick, named Lazarus, of Bethany, the town of Mary and her sister Martha.

(It was that Mary which anointed the Lord with ointment, and wiped His feet with her hair, whose brother Lazarus was sick.)

Therefore his sisters sent unto Him, saying, Lord, behold, he whom thou lovest is sick.

When Jesus heard that, He said, This sickness is not unto death, but for the glory of God, that the Son of God might be glorified thereby.

In this scripture someone calls upon the name of the Lord, interceding for a man whom they bring, who is deaf and dumb.

Mark 7:32-35

And they bring unto Him one that was deaf, and had an impediment in his speech; and they beseech Him to put His hand upon him.

And He took him aside from the multitude, and put His fingers into his ears, and he spit, and touched his tongue;

And looking up to heaven, He sighed, and saith unto him, Ephphatha, that is, Be opened.

And straightway his ears were opened, and the string of his tongue was loosed, and he spake plain.

Each time a person called upon the name of the Lord, He answered, and He showed to them great and mighty things. We cannot hear God answer if we don't believe that He is. We cannot hear God answer if we have not trained our ears to hear His voice. We cannot hear God if we concern ourselves with the things of the world more than we concern ourselves with God's word.

God shared with me this week that you can know the heart of a man or woman by their conversation. There are three different types of conversations.

1. The conversations of those in the world (those who know nothing of Christ).
2. The conversations of those who have confessed Christ but have not renewed their minds and still retain the conversation of the world.

3.   The conversations of those who have confessed Christ, who have renewed their minds in the word of God, and have sold out to God.

Of the first two, they hear the voice of God, but fail to obey Him. The third hear His slightest whisper and obey His every word.

What type of conversations do you have?

CHAPTER 2

God Commands That We Hear His Voice

Mark 12:28-31; Deuteronomy 6:4; Revelation 2:17

What is the first commandment?

When Moses reiterates the Law to the people in Deuteronomy 5; 6, he begins by saying, Hear, O Israel! Moses is the spokes person for God, he is saying what God has told him to say, just the way God would say it. And he says:

Deuteronomy 6:4, 5
Hear, O Israel: The Lord our God is one Lord:
And thou shalt love the Lord thy God with all thine heart, and with all thy soul, and with all thy might

When Jesus was asked, What is the **first** commandment (not the greatest commandment), He answers with the same command that Moses gave.

Mark 12:28-31
And one of the scribes came, and having heard them reasoning together, and perceiving that He had answered them well, asked Him, Which is the first commandment of all?
And Jesus answered him, The first of all the commandments is, **Hear, O Israel**; The Lord our God is one Lord:
And thou shalt love the Lord thy God with all thy heart, and with all thy soul, and with all thy mind, and with all thy strength: this is the first commandment.
And the second is like, namely this, Thou shalt love thy neighbor as thyself. There is none other commandment greater than these.

Abraham heard God and obeyed. There was no prophet there to tell Abraham what God was saying. There was no priest there to tell him what God was saying. Abraham heard God for himself.

Genesis 12:1-4
Now **the Lord had said unto Abram**, Get thee out of thy country, and from thy kindred, and from thy father's house, unto a land that I will show thee:
And I will make of thee a great nation, and I will bless thee, and make thy name great; and thou shalt be a blessing:
And I will bless them that bless thee, and curse him that curseth thee: and in thee shall all families of the earth be blessed.

So Abram departed, **as the Lord had spoken unto him**; and Lot went with him: and Abram was seventy and five years old when he departed out of Haran.

So many times I have had different ones to tell me about a dream that they'd had, or a vision, in which God was giving them instructions to do or to say something. But they wait on their pastors or some prophet to tell them again, or to let them know what God meant. It is ok to get confirmation, but we must learn to trust God when He first speaks.

Many times God will be saying to them, It is time to go, time to leave this ministry. Or He will say, It is time for you to separate from these people. But the one who heard God speak waits for the very one that God is telling them to get away from to confirm what God is saying.

God told Abraham to leave his father and his father's house. But he tried to take his father with him (Genesis 11:31). God did not want Abraham's father to go with him into the promised land, because Terah still worshiped idols (Nachor was Abraham's brother). Many times the people that God is telling you to get away from are worshiping idols. God is a jealous God!

Joshua 24:2

And Joshua said unto all the people, Thus saith the Lord God of Israel, Your fathers dwelt on the other side of the flood in old time, even Terah, the father of Abraham, and the father of Nachor: and they served other gods.

God will speak to us in dreams and visions, but He would rather speak to us face to face, as He spoke to Moses. But many times we will not take the time to spend with God, nor do we take the time to learn His language. Still God has a way of getting our attention. In this scripture, unlike at other times Aaron and Miriam heard God's voice instead of having a dream or a vision.

Numbers 12:4-8

And the Lord spake suddenly unto Moses, and unto Aaron, and unto Miriam, Come out ye three unto the tabernacle of the congregation. And they three came out.

And the Lord came down in the pillar of the cloud, and stood in the door of the tabernacle, and called Aaron and Miriam: and they both came forth.

And He said, Hear now my words: If there be a prophet among you, I the Lord will make myself known unto him in a vision, and will speak unto him in a dream.

My servant Moses is not so, who is faithful in all mine house.

With him will I speak mouth to mouth, even apparently, and not in dark speeches; and the similitude of the Lord shall he behold: wherefore then were ye not afraid to speak against my servant Moses?

Aaron and Miriam had to be tired and warn out before they would be still long enough to hear from God; and then in dreams and visions. But Moses had become a very humble and patient man after leaving Egypt. He had learned to obey God's slightest whisper.

The word hearken means to **hear and obey**. God promises that if we will obey His voice, He will dwell with us, love, and protect us. Obedience towards God is a sign of your love for Him.

Exodus 15:26

And said, If thou wilt diligently **hearken to the voice of the Lord thy God**, and wilt do that which is right in His sight, and wilt give ear to His commandments, and keep all His statutes, I will put none of these diseases upon thee, which I have brought upon the Egyptians: for I am the Lord that healeth thee.

Deuteronomy 7:12-15

Wherefore it shall come to pass, if ye hearken to these judgments, and keep, and do them, that the Lord thy God shall keep unto thee the covenant and the mercy which He sware unto thy fathers:

And He will love thee, and bless thee, and multiply thee: He will also bless the fruit of thy womb, and the fruit of thy land, thy corn, and thy wine, and thine oil, the increase of thy kine, and the flocks of thy sheep, in the land which He sware unto thy fathers to give thee.

Thou shalt be blessed above all people: there shall not be male or female barren among you, or among your cattle.

And the Lord will take away from thee all sickness, and will put none of the evil diseases of Egypt, which thou knowest, upon thee; but will lay them upon all them that hate thee.

Jesus said,

John 14:15, 23-24

If ye love me, keep my commandments.
(keep-hearken, hear and obey)

v. 23, 24

Jesus answered and said unto him, If a man love me, he will keep my words: and my Father will love him, and we will come unto him, and make our abode with him.

He that loveth me not keepeth not my sayings: and the word which ye hear is not mine, but the Father's which sent me.

One of the first things that Jesus experienced, after He came out of the water, when John baptized Him, was to hear the voice of God.

Mark 1: 9-11

And it came to pass in those days, that Jesus came from Nazareth of Galilee, and was baptized of John in Jordan.

And straightway coming up out of the water, He saw the heavens opened, and the Spirit like a dove descending upon Him:

And there came a voice from heaven, saying, Thou art my beloved Son, in whom I am well pleased.

Jesus heard God's voice and obeyed Him. Jesus never spoke outside of the words that He heard God speak.

John 12:47-50

And if any man hear my words, and believe not, I judge him not: for I came not to judge the world, but to save the world.

He that rejecteth me, and receiveth not my words, hath one that judgeth him: the word that I have spoken, the same shall judge him in the last day.

For I have not spoken of myself; but the Father which sent me, He gave me a commandment, what I should say, and what I should speak.

And I know that His commandment is life everlasting: whatsoever I speak therefore, even as the Father said unto me, so I speak.

Jesus never did anything except He saw His Father do it.

John 5:19-21

Then answered Jesus and said unto them, Verily, verily, I say unto you, The Son can do nothing of Himself, but what He seeth the Father do: **for what things soever He doeth, these also doeth the Son likewise.**

For the Father loveth the Son, and showeth Him all things that Himself doeth: and He will show Him greater works than these, that ye may marvel.

For as the Father raiseth up the dead, and quickeneth them; even so the Son quickeneth whom He will.

Jesus teaches His disciples to hear the voice of God. The first to learn to hear was Peter. The only way that Peter could have known that Jesus was the Christ is that God had spoken it to him. In Jesus calling Simon by the name Peter, He is giving to us a very important key. For the name Peter means a stone. In teaching them to hear the voice of God, Jesus is giving to them the keys to the kingdom of heaven. To hear God's voice is the foundation of the church.

Matthew 16:15-19

He saith unto them, But whom say ye that I am?
And Simon Peter answered and said, Thou art the Christ, the Son of the living God.

And Jesus answered and said unto him, Blessed art thou, Simon Bar-jona: for flesh and blood hath not revealed it unto thee, but my Father which is in heaven.

And I say also unto thee, That thou art Peter, and upon this rock I will build my church; and the gates of hell shall not prevail against it.

And I will give unto thee the keys of the kingdom of heaven: and whatsoever thou shalt bind on earth shall be bound in heaven: and whatsoever thou shall loose on earth shall be loosed in heaven.

Next, Jesus teaches His disciples that there is more than one voice. He uses Peter to do this, that He might teach them all a lesson. Like us, the disciples had to experience a thing before they understood it.

Peter had received a new gift, he had learned to hear God's voice. He mistakenly thought that every voice that he heard was God.

Jesus knows this because what Peter says is contrary to what the word of God says. This is why it is so important that each of us study daily the word of God. The Bible says that the Lamb was slain. Peter contradicts this when he rebukes Jesus. He contradicts it because he is listening to the devil's voice. Let us see this in action.

Matthew 16:21-24

From that time forth began Jesus to show unto His disciples, how that He must go unto Jerusalem, and suffer many things of the elders and chief priests and scribes, and be killed, and be raised again the third day.

Then Peter took Him, and began to rebuke Him, saying, Be it far from thee, Lord: this shall not be unto thee.

But He turned, and said unto Peter, Get thee behind me, Satan: thou art an offense unto me: for thou savorest not the things that be of God, but those that be of men.

Then said Jesus unto His disciples, If any man will come after me, let him deny himself, and take up his cross, and follow me.

Within six days James and John have learned to hear God's voice along with Peter; and Jesus takes the three of them along with Him to pray. This time they not only see in the spirit, they hear God's audible voice.

Matthew 17:1-6

And after six days Jesus taketh Peter, James, and John his brother, and bringeth them up into a high mountain apart,

And was transfigured before them: and His face did shine as the sun, and His raiment was white as the light.

And, behold, there appeared unto them Moses and Elijah talking with Him.

Then answered Peter, and said unto Jesus, Lord, it is good for us to be here: if thou wilt, let us make here three tabernacles; one for thee, and one for Moses, and one for Elijah.

While he yet spake, behold, a bright cloud overshadowed them: **and behold a voice out of the cloud, which said,** This is my beloved Son, in whom I am well pleased; **hear ye Him**.

And when the disciples heard it they fell on their face, and were sore afraid.

Why was it that Peter, James and John were the ones taken and not the other nine?

If you can remember, Peter, Andrew, James and John were fishing partners. Jesus called James and John, Boanerges, the son's of thunder: because they were boasters, and would brag about how well they could fish, and do anything else.

Peter being their partner, had learned something that they did not know. So, within six days, James and John had fasted and prayed, and learned to hear God's voice too. They were not going to allow Peter to out do them.

The reason Jesus took the three of them is because they now have faith, and were now ready for the next experience, to also see in the spirit.

The other nine disciples didn't believe that one could hear God's voice (as many in the church today). In separating Peter, James, and John, Jesus is teaching the other nine disciples the importance of fasting and praying, and hearing the voice of God.

Matthew 17:14-21

And when they were come to the multitude, there came to Him a certain man, kneeling down to Him, and saying,

Lord, have mercy on my son: for he is lunatic, and sore vexed: for ofttimes he falleth into the fire, and oft into the water.

And I brought him to thy disciples, and they could not cure him.

Then Jesus answered and said, O faithless and perverse generation, how long shall I be with you? How long shall I suffer you? Bring him hither to me.

And Jesus rebuked the devil; and he departed out of him: and the child was cured from that very hour.

Then came the disciples to Jesus apart, and said, Why could not we cast him out?

And Jesus said unto them, **Because of your unbelief**: for verily I say unto you, If ye **have faith** as a grain of mustard seed, ye shall say unto this mountain, Remove hence to yonder place; and it shall remove; and nothing shall be impossible unto you.

Howbeit this kind goeth not out but by prayer and fasting.

When Jesus called them a faithless and perverse generation, He was speaking of the nine more so than unto the multitude that had gathered. For it was the nine who had not believed that Peter, James and John could hear the voice of God.

It was the nine who asked Jesus, Why could we not cast him out? Not Peter, James and John.

The nine had always depended upon Jesus to instruct them. But when the man comes to them with his son, Jesus was away. Jesus wants them to learn to depend on God and not always on Jesus' presence. Throughout the Bible, the reason men fasted and prayed was to quiet their body and mind that they could hear God's voice, and receive instructions from Him.

Note another thing, these twelve disciples had been out preaching the gospel. Yet they had not learned how to hear the voice of God. They were only repeating what they had heard Jesus say. And if they were only repeating what they heard Jesus say, then, did they really understand the gospel? When you take a close look at the four gospels, the writers themselves will admit that they did not understand until after the day of Pentecost, when they all heard God's voice.

In 1997 a woman told me about a dream she'd had. In the dream there was a pole with a beautiful parakeet perched on top. It was just sitting there atop the pole. Nothing else was going on in the dream. So she asked the Lord, saying, What does this mean? He said, What do you see? She answered, A parakeet. He said, What is it doing? She answered, Sitting on top of a pole. And she noted that there was a chain connecting the parakeet and the pole.

The next morning she got up and looked up the word parakeet. The definition said, A beautifully feathered bird that can mock men perfectly without understanding what it is saying.

The Lord then reminded her of the pole. The pole resembled a cross without a head. He said to her, Too many pastors in my church today are just like that parakeet. They can perfectly quote my word but they have no understanding. They are chained, in bondage to the churches that they pastor, which have not Jesus Christ as the head. That chain is money, fame, and power.

The nine disciples did not believe that Peter could hear the voice of God, therefore they had no faith. When they had preached before, they were only repeating what they'd heard Jesus say. Jesus repeatedly kept telling them that He was going to leave them: which meant that they needed to learn how to hear God's voice for themselves. By depending on the man Jesus, they had no need to hear God's voice. Until this point, they believed that God is, and that God had sent Jesus; but they did not believe that one could talk with God.

Belief and faith are two different things. You can believe a thing and not have faith in it. To believe in God is one thing, but to hear God and obey is faith.

Romans 10:17

So then faith cometh by hearing, and hearing by the word of God.

Hearing the voice of God sometimes means that God is speaking directly to you, as He spoke to Ananias.

Acts 9:8-12

And Saul arose from the earth; and when his eyes were opened, he saw no man: but they led him by the hand, and brought him into Damascus.

And he was three days without sight, and neither did eat nor drink.

And there was a certain disciple at Damascus, named Ananias; and to him said the Lord in a vision, Ananias. And he said, Behold, I am here, Lord.

And the Lord said unto him, Arise, and go into the street which is called Straight, and inquire in the house of Judas for one called Saul of Tarsus: for, behold, he prayeth,

And hath seen in a vision a man named Ananias coming in, and putting his hand on him, that he might receive his sight.

Hearing the voice of God sometimes means that God will speak to you through another person, as Ananias spoke to Paul. Usually this is to confirm His word. This allowed Paul to know that it was the Lord who told him that Ananias was coming, and what he would say and do.

Ananias told Paul that he would hear the voice of the Lord.

Acts 22:14-15

And he said, The God of our Fathers hath chosen thee, that thou shouldest know His will, and see that Just One, **and shouldest hear the voice of His mouth.**

For thou shalt be His witness unto all men of what thou hast seen and heard.

Jesus says that those who hear and obey God's words are wise.

Matthew 7:24-27

Therefore whosoever heareth these sayings of mine, and doeth them, I will liken him unto a wise man, which built his house upon a rock:

And the rain descended, and the floods came, and the winds blew, and beat upon that house; and it fell not; for it was founded upon a rock.

And every one that heareth these sayings of mine, and doeth them not, shall be likened unto a foolish man, which built his house upon the sand:

And the rain descended, and the floods came, and the winds blew, and beat upon that house; and it fell: and great was the fall of it.

A major key to the kingdom of God is to hear the voice of God. It is the Stone, the Rock, the foundation in which the kingdom is built upon.

Matthew 16:18, 19

And I say also unto thee, That thou art Peter, and upon this **rock I will build my church**; and the gates of hell shall not prevail against it.

And I will give unto thee the keys of the kingdom of heaven: and whatsoever thou shalt bind on earth shall be bound in heaven: and whatsoever thou shalt loose on earth shall be loosed in heaven.

Throughout the Bible when you see the words rock or stone, it is speaking of someone hearing the voice of God.

Jesus named Simon by the name Peter (Matthew 16:18), which means a stone, a rock. So does the name Cephas (John 1:42).

The Ten Commandments were written upon two stone tablets, representing the fact that the children of Israel all heard God's voice (Deuteronomy 5:22).

In Genesis 28:10-22, Jacob laid on the rock to sleep for the night, and he heard the voice of God; for the word says that God spoke to him. In other words, he "fell on" that rock.

It was the law when one was disobedient for certain crimes that the person was put to death by stoning (Deuteronomy 17:5; Joshua 7:25). In this case the stone is "falling upon him" and grinding him to powder. That person had disobeyed God's voice.

This is what Jesus was speaking of when He gave the parable of the builders rejecting the corner stone.

Matthew 21:42-46

Jesus saith unto them, Did ye never read in the Scriptures, The stone which the builders rejected, the same is become the head of the corner: this is the Lord's doing, and it is marvelous in our eyes?

Therefore say I unto you, The kingdom of God shall be taken from you, and given to a nation bringing forth the fruits thereof.

And whosoever shall fall on this stone shall be broken: but on whomsoever it shall fall, it will grind him to powder.

And when the chief priests and Pharisees had heard His parables, they perceived that He spake of them.

But when they sought to lay hands on Him, they feared the multitude, because they took Him for a prophet.

Many times since the Lord called me into the ministry I have come up against many pastors and ministers who do not believe that one can hear the voice of God. Yet they say they were called by God to preach the gospel of Jesus Christ.

This lets me know that they do not have the keys to the kingdom of heaven.
Nor have they experienced their Pentecost; because they have rejected the corner stone.

God said to me, Hearing the voice of God is the foundation of the church! Teaching men to do so is the responsibility of all ministers of the Gospel of Jesus
Christ. Woe, to any pastor, evangelist, prophet, apostle, or teacher who refuses to teach God's people how to hear His voice!

Matthew 23:13

But woe unto you, scribes and Pharisees, hypocrites! For ye shut up the kingdom of heaven against men: for ye neither go in yourselves, neither suffer ye them that enter to go in.

I Peter 2:4-8

To whom coming, as unto a living stone, disallowed indeed of men, but chosen of God, and precious,

Ye also, as lively stones, are built up a spiritual house, a holy priesthood, to offer up spiritual sacrifices, acceptable to God by Jesus Christ.

Wherefore also it is contained in the Scripture, Behold, I lay in Zion a chief corner stone, elect, precious: and he that believeth on Him shall not be confounded.

Unto you therefore which believe He is precious: but unto them which be disobedient, the stone which the builders disallowed, the same is made the head of the corner,

And a stone of stumbling, and a rock of offense, even to them which stumble at the word, being disobedient: whereunto also they were appointed.

Hearing God's voice and being obedient is the rock, the stone, the foundation of the church; the foundation of the city, New Jerusalem; the foundation of the apostles and prophets.

Matthew 16:18

And I say also unto thee, That thou art Peter, and upon this **rock I will build my church**; and the gates of hell shall not prevail against it.

Ephesians 2:20

And are built upon **the foundation of the apostles and prophets**, Jesus Christ Himself being the chief corner stone. (What did they have in common?)

Revelation 21:10-20

And he carried me away in the spirit to a great and high mountain, and showed me that great city, the holy Jerusalem, descending out of heaven from God,

Having the glory of God: and her light was like unto a stone most precious, even like a jasper stone, clear as crystal;

And had a wall great and high, and had twelve gates, and at the gates twelve angels, and names written thereon, which are the names of the twelve tribes of the children of Israel:

On the east three gates; on the north three gates; on the south three gates; and on the west three gates.

And the wall of the city had **twelve foundations**, and in them the names of the twelve apostles of the Lamb.

And he that talked with me had a golden reed to measure the city, and the gates thereof, and the wall thereof.

And the city lieth foursquare, and the length is as large as the breadth: and he measured the city with the reed, twelve thousand furlongs. The length and the breadth and the height of it are equal.

And he measured the wall thereof, a hundred and forty and four cubits, according to the measure of a man, that is, of the angel.

And the building of the wall of it was of jasper: and the city was pure gold, like unto clear glass.

And **the foundations of the wall of the city** were garnished with all manner of **precious stones**. The first foundation was jasper; the second, sapphire; the third, a chalcedony; the fourth, an emerald;

The fifth, sardonyx; the sixth, sardius; the seventh, chrysolyte; the eighth, beryl; the ninth, a topaz; the tenth, a chrysoprasus; the eleventh, a jacinth; the twelfth, an amethyst.

Throughout the Gospels and the book of Revelation, Jesus says, He that hath an ear, **let him hear what the Spirit saith** (Matthew 11:15; 13:9, 43; Mark 4:9; Luke 8:8; Revelation 2:7, 11, 17, 29; 3:6, 13, 22; 13:9).

God calls many to build His church, for many are called but few are chosen. But why are they not chosen?

Because many refuse to seek God to find out just what the foundation is. They try to build their ministries on the foundations of others, what others have done and said (tradition).

Jonathan the son of Saul was a mighty man of God: he could hear God's voice. Knowing that his father was wrong, yet out of honor and respect for his father, he followed Saul to his death. Be careful of following traditions.

Still others heard God, but refuse to obey His voice, and begin to build, but doing it their own way. The love of money, power, and fame will ruin a ministry.

In Matthew 4:1-11, then was Jesus tempted by Satan with power, fame, and money. But Jesus passed the test. If Jesus was tempted, how do you think that you won't be? And when you are tempted, will you know what is happening to you? Will you pass the test, or fall in the snare?

King Saul fell in the snare, and he was rejected by God.

I Samuel 15:22, 23

And Samuel said, Hath the Lord as great delight in burnt offerings and sacrifices, as in obeying the voice of the Lord? Behold, to obey is better than sacrifice, and to hearken than the fat of rams.

For rebellion is as the sin of witchcraft, and stubbornness is as iniquity and idolatry. Because thou hast rejected the word of the Lord, He hath also rejected thee from being king.

Except God instruct you in building the ministry in which He has called you to, you are building it in vain. The only way He can instruct you is that you hear His voice and obey.

Psalm 127:1

Except the Lord build the house, they labor in vain that build it: except the Lord keep the city, the watchman waketh but in vain.

God had sent the exiles back to Jerusalem to rebuild the temple, but after they arrived they began to build their own homes and vineyards instead, but were not prosperous. It was not until the prophet Haggai prophesied to them, warning them that they should build God's temple first; and they obeyed, then they began to prosper.

God reminded them of this, saying,

Haggai 2:15-19

And now, I pray you, consider from this day and upward, from before a stone was laid upon a stone in the temple of the Lord:

Since those days were, when one came to an heap of twenty measures, there were but ten: when one came to the wine vat for to draw out fifty vessels out of the press, there were but twenty.

I smote you with blasting and with mildew and with hail in all the labors of your hands; yet ye turned not to me, saith the Lord.

Consider now from this day and upward, from the four and twentieth day of the ninth month, even from the day that the foundation of the Lord's temple was laid, consider it.

Is the seed yet in the barn? Yea, as yet the vine, and the fig tree, and the pomegranate, and the olive tree, hath not brought forth: from this day will I bless you.

The temple of God today is not a building, nor is it an organization, but your heart.

I Corinthians 3:16

Know ye not that ye are the temple of God, and that the Spirit of God dwelleth in you?

II Corinthians 6:16

And what agreement hath the temple of God with idols? For ye are the temple of the living God; as God hath said, I will dwell in them, and walk in them; and I will be their God, and they shall be my people.

Are you willing to put aside your own plans, that you may have time to spend with God, learning how to hear His voice and to walk in obedience to His every word?

CHAPTER 3

It All Begins With A Testimony!
Luke 17:11-19

In the weeks to come we will be studying about Hearing the voice of God, the Ten Commandments, and Foundational Truths. To begin we study the testimony. In this lesson we will learn the importance of hearing the voice of God and being obedient.

What is a testimony?

A testimony is a statement made based on one's direct knowledge that coincides with another's; a witness to the words of another.

A preacher bases what he or she says on his or her own direct knowledge of the experiences of Jesus.

You cannot tell a thing in truth until you have experienced it for yourself. You cannot tell another's story properly until you have had the same experience.

Now let us look at this scripture to better understand what a testimony is.

Luke 17:11-19

And it came to pass, as he went to Jerusalem, that he passed through the midst of Samaria and Galilee.

And as he entered into a certain village, there met him ten men that were lepers, which stood afar off:

And they lifted up their voices, and said, Jesus, Master, have mercy on us.

And when he saw them, he said unto them, Go show yourselves unto the priests. And it came to pass, that, as they went, they were cleansed.

And one of them, when he saw that he was healed, turned back, and with a loud voice glorified God,

And fell down on his face at his feet, giving him thanks: and he was a Samaritan.

And Jesus answering said, Were there not ten cleansed? but where are the nine?

There are not found that returned to give glory to God, save this stranger.

And he said unto him, Arise, go thy way: thy faith hath made thee whole.

In sending the lepers to the priests, Jesus is asking them to be witnesses to the gospel. Note that this one man is not a Jew but a Samaritan, and Jesus calls him a stranger in verse 18. Even this man being not a Jew, called upon the name of the Lord, and he was healed.

The Bible says that God has no respect of person. The Bible says, For whosoever shall call upon the name of the Lord shall be saved (Romans 10:13). The Bible also says, For this is good and acceptable in the sight of God our Savior; who will have all men to be saved, and to come unto the knowledge of the truth (I Timothy 2:3, 4).

It is not God's desire that any man be sick, nor is it His desire that any man go to hell. It is God's desire that each of us be healed (saved, delivered), and that each of us be made whole (receive salvation, eternal life). He also wants each of us to come into the knowledge of the truth (to see, and to enter into the kingdom of God).

The truth is that God loves us so much that He wants each of us to be able to come into the kingdom of God, the Garden of Eden; which means that each of us will have a personal relationship with Him. And in coming into this relationship, each of us will be willing to tell others who are lost about the kingdom. This is the good news, this is the Gospel!

In this relationship, you learn that God is your protection, your provider, your healer, your guide, your comforter, and your teacher. Everything you need, you have in God. He said that He will be "all things to you." He said, I Am That, I Am!

God is God of His word, He keeps His promises, that is what the name Jehovah means.

All He wants from us is that we love Him with our whole heart. In loving Him, you obey Him. Jesus said in John 14:15, If you love me keep my commandments. Now this is where faith comes in.

To obey God we must hear Him. And when we hear His voice, we obey what He says, whether written or spoken. Whether you hear Him for yourself or someone else has to speak it to you. Eventually you must learn to hear Him for yourself.

A relationship with God begins with hearing His voice. It takes faith to believe the word that you hear. Faith comes by hearing, and hearing by the word of God (Romans 10:17). We can believe that God speaks to us, but faith kicks in when we obey what He says. The devils believe and tremble that God is (James 2:19), but they don't obey Him. That is why they are doomed for the lake that burns with fire and brimstone.

Let us look at the process of loving God, in Luke 17:11-19.

The lepers all cried out to Jesus in faith, asking Him to heal them. But when He did not lay hands on them to heal them, but simply said to them, Go to the priests; the lepers obeyed in faith, His word.

And as they were going, they were healed. It was not the offering that healed them, it was their obedience to the word Jesus spoke.
He did not say to them, go make the sacrifice that Moses commanded, because the nine of them already knew; because they were Jews. They knew that a leper, when healed was to go show himself to the priests and take an offering, because it is written in the law (Leviticus 14:1, 2). Jesus simply said, Go, show yourselves unto the priests.

Too many Christians have no faith in the word, and refuse to simply obey God's word because of fear. Fear is a spirit. The Bible says, For God has not given to us the spirit of fear; but of power, and of love, and of a sound mind (II Timothy 1:7). Fear comes from the devil.

It is up to us to overcome this spirit of fear. We overcome it by simply obeying God: it is then that faith comes. Again, we receive faith when we obey God's word, whether written or spoken.

Faith is the substance of things hoped for, the evidence of things not seen. For by it the elders had a good report (Hebrews 11:1, 2).

The elders had a good report because they heard God's voice and they obeyed.

The Bible says, Without faith it is impossible to please God. If you don't have faith in God's word, then you are walking in disobedience.

Romans 10:17-21

So then faith cometh by hearing, and hearing by the word of God.

But I say, Have they not heard? Yes very, their sound went into all the earth, and their words unto the ends of the world.

But I say, Did not Israel know? First Moses saith, I will provoke you to jealousy by them that are no people, and by a foolish nation I will anger you.

But Isaiah is very bold, and saith, I was found of them that sought me not; I was made manifest unto them that asked not after me.

But to Israel he saith, All day long I have stretched forth my hands unto a disobedient and gainsaying people.

Israel did not believe God, whether He spoke by Moses or by Isaiah.

Of the ten lepers, nine of them knew the law concerning the offering of a leper, therefore Jesus only had to say, Go, show yourselves unto the priests. The nine knew the law but had no understanding of it.

But this one man, the stranger, did not know the law, he did not know why he was going to take an offering. So, he asked the others, Why go show ourselves to the priests? They answered; We have to take an offering. The stranger then asked, What kind of offering are we to take? And they told him that a leper who has been cleansed is to bring two turtle doves, cedar wood, scarlet, and hyssop (Leviticus 14:1-4).

Then the stranger asked the others, And what does this sacrifice mean?

They could only tell him what the law says. But they could not give him the understanding of the law. In knowing the law they had wisdom, but they lacked understanding.

The Bible says, The fear (obedience) of the Lord is the beginning of wisdom (Proverbs 9:10). The Bible also says, Wisdom is the principal thing; therefore get wisdom: and with all thy getting get understanding (Proverbs 4:7).

And where do we get understanding?

The Bible says, If any of you lack wisdom, let him ask of God, that giveth to all men liberally, and upbraideth not; and it shall be given him (James 1:5; Deuteronomy 4:6).

Again, the man, speaking within himself, asks, What does this sacrifice mean? And he heard the voice of God answer. God told him to do something. The thing God told the man to do was to return to Jesus, and thank Him. And the man obeyed.

But when the man turned to go back to Jesus, something happened. The Spirit of the Lord came upon him, for the Bible says that he turned back, and with a loud voice glorified God, and fell down on his face at his feet, giving Him thanks.

It hurt Jesus because the nine Hebrew men did not return after they had seen that they were healed. They were stuck in tradition. Yet it delighted Him because this one man, a stranger, a Samaritan, did return. It was not because he said thank you to Jesus, that delighted Him, but because Jesus knew that this man had heard the voice of God and obeyed.

The meaning of the sacrifice was just what the man did, he obeyed God, and he thanked Jesus, who is the High Priest.

This is why Jesus said to the man, Arise, go thy way: thy faith hath made thee whole. Jesus did not tell him to go to the priests, but to go his way. For in obeying the voice of God, the man had already offered his sacrifice. This man had gained the understanding of the offerings. It is not the animal sacrifice that God desires, it is obedience, and the sacrifice of your lips.

I Samuel 15:22, 23

And Samuel said, Hath the Lord as great delight in burnt offerings and sacrifices, as in obeying the voice of the Lord? Behold, to obey is better than sacrifice, and to hearken than the fat of rams.

For rebellion is as the sin of witchcraft, and stubbornness is as iniquity and idolatry. Because thou hast rejected the word of the Lord, He hath also rejected thee from being king.

In the year 2000 there were four women attending a Foundation Truths class that I was teaching in my home. One of them had a daughter who was very close to her. The two of them went every where together. Although the daughter was invited to come to the classes, she refused.

One evening she did come. She told us that she had been jealous of her mother's excitement about attending the classes. On this particular night she was led to come, and bring along her one year old son with her.

We began the class as usual, and at the close of the class we gathered in a circle, holding hands to pray. At the end of the prayer the Lord told me to turn towards my front door. I did. And He spoke to me saying, Tell the young woman to say, Thank You Jesus!

I asked why and He told me. Then I turned to the young woman and told her what God had said. She said, Why? I told her that God had said that when she was in the hospital delivering her son that she had almost died, because she also had lupus. Your mother, your sister, and your aunt had interceded for you. And you lived, but you never told the Lord, Thank You.

And she thought on it for a moment and then said, You are right. She then lifted up her head and said aloud, Thank you Jesus!

As soon as she said the words, the Spirit of the Lord fell upon her, and she began to praise the Lord, aloud!

The Lord told me to turn to the door again, and I did. This time He said, Tell her that I sent her here this evening. Tell her that I am calling her into the ministry to preach the gospel.

I turned to her and told her what the Lord had said. She just looked at me. Then the Lord told me to tell her that she already knows this. I told her, and she gasped and cupped her hands to her mouth. The other women in the room and I knew by her reaction that the Lord had called her and she had known it.

She confirmed it, and said that she had heard the Lord speaking to her but she was not sure because no one had told her that she could hear the voice of God before.

The Lord then told me to turn to the door again, and I did. This time He told me to tell the mother of this young woman to lay hands on her daughter and cast out the spirit of sickness, the lupus, to leave her daughter. She did, and her daughter was healed. To this day she has not taken any medication, nor has she had any symptoms of the disease.

When the young woman had delivered her son she had lupus, causing the baby to be born premature. And at a year old he was very small for his age. He had begun to walk, but he walked on his tip toes. The Lord told the grandmother to pray for him that night too. She did, and he too was healed.

Unlike the other nine, this Samaritan had believed the voice of the Lord, he had been obedient. Yes, God had spoken to each of them, but only this stranger had obeyed what he heard. And because of his obedience, he not only received healing in his body, but he received eternal life. To be whole means to have eternal life.

This Samaritan, who had been a leper, now has a testimony. His testimony came not because he was healed, but because he heard God and obeyed. His testimony is not just the fact that he was healed, but having received wholeness, which includes the fact that he would rise from the dead, just as Jesus rose from the dead. His testimony was that he obeyed God's voice.

Jesus had told the men to go to the priests. They were to offer the sacrifice that Moses had commanded, **as a testimony unto the priests**.

The testimony that this man now has is the same testimony that John wrote of in the book of Revelation.

Revelation 12:11

And they overcame him (Satan) by the blood of the Lamb, and by the word of their testimony; and they loved not their lives unto the death.

You can only overcome Satan by focusing on Jesus and the fact that He obeyed God's every word; even unto death, even the death of the cross.

You too can have the same testimony as Jesus, if you will hear God's voice and obey. Obey God even in your sickness, even in your persecutions, even in your trials and temptations. You must trust God so much that you obey His every word, even if it cost you your life.

This is the love of God. There is no fear in love; but perfect love casteth out fear: because fear hath torment. He that feareth is not made perfect in love (I John 4:18).

Even if you face death because of your obedience, there is no fear when you have faith in God. Because you know that the same God who raised up Jesus Christ from the dead, will also raise you up from the dead.

This is the same testimony that Job had when he said, For I know that my Redeemer liveth, and that He shall stand at the latter day upon the earth: and though after my skin worms destroy this body, yet in my flesh shall I see God: Whom I shall see for myself, and mine eyes shall behold, and not another; though my reins be consumed within me (Job 19:25-27).

This is the same testimony that the three Hebrew men had when they stood before king Nebuchadnezzar and the fiery furnace.

Daniel 3:16-18

Shadrach, Meshach, and Abed-nego, answered and said to the king, O Nebuchadnezzar, we are not careful to answer thee in this matter.

If it be so, our God whom we serve is able to deliver us from the burning fiery furnace, and He will deliver us out of thine hand, O king.

But if not, be it known unto thee, O king, that we will not serve thy gods, nor worship the golden image which thou hast set up.

God wants each of us to have this kind of faith in Him. He wants us to be witnesses of His love and mercy. You cannot simply tell others the story of Jesus and His faith in God, you too must have that same faith. You too must have this testimony.

To get this testimony you too must be tried in the fire, and tested. For this is the Gospel! This is the good news! To have been through the trial, and trusted in the love of God to deliver you!

Are you willing to be obedient to God's every word, whether written, or spoken, even if it cost you your life?????

CHAPTER 4

How To Minister To God

God is crying out to His children!   See God's heart!

Hosea 11:1-12

When Israel was a child, then I loved him, and called my son out of Egypt.

As they called them, so they went from them: they sacrificed unto Baalim, and burned incense to graven images.

I taught Ephraim also to go, taking them by their arms; but they knew not that I healed them.

I drew them with cords of a man, with bands of love: and I was to them as they that take off the yoke on their jaws, and I laid meat unto them.

He shall not return into the land of Egypt, but the Assyrian shall be his king, because they refused to return.

And the sword shall abide on his cities, and shall consume his branches, and devour them, because of their own counsels.

And my people are bent to backsliding from me: though they called them to the most High, none at all would exalt Him.

How shall I give thee up, Ephraim? how shall I deliver thee, Israel? how shall I make thee as Admah? how shall I set thee as Zeboim? **Mine heart is turned within me, my repentings are kindled together.**

I will not execute the fierceness of mine anger, I will not return to destroy Ephraim: for I am God, and not man; the Holy One in the midst of thee: and I will not enter into the city.

They shall walk after the Lord: **He shall roar like a lion: when He shall roar, then the children shall tremble from the west.**

They shall tremble as a bird out of Egypt, and as a dove out of the land of Assyria: and I will place them in their houses, saith the Lord.

Ephraim compasseth me about with lies, and the house of Israel with deceit: but Judah yet ruleth with God, and is faithful with the saints.

Mary ministers to Jesus.

Luke 7:36-50 (44-48)

And He turned to the woman, and said unto Simon, Seest thou this woman? I entered into thine house, thou gavest me no water for my feet: but she hath washed my feet with the hair of her head.

Thou gavest me no kiss: but this woman since the time I came in, hath not ceased to kiss my feet.

My head with oil thou didst not anoint: but this woman hath anointed my feet with ointment.

Wherefore I say unto thee, Her sins, which are many, are forgiven; **for she loved much**: but to whom little is forgiven, the same loveth little.

And He said unto her, Thy sins are forgiven.

It was tradition that the women eat in a separate room when there were guest. It was tradition for a woman to let her hair down only in the presence of her husband. It was tradition for a single woman without children to purchase the expensive, but fragrant oil for her own burial. Mary broke these traditions. Mary did this because God told her to. Not because she knew that Jesus was going to be crucified.

Because Mary was not afraid to show forth her love, Jesus said she shall always be remembered. Not just for her glory, but as an example to us, an example of how to humble yourself before the feet of God.

Matthew 26:13

Verily I say unto you, Wheresoever this gospel shall be preached in the whole world, there shall also this, that this woman hath done, be told for a memorial of her.

So then, how do we minister to God?

Get alone by yourself, put on worship music: music that blesses the name of the Lord. Listen to the words, then begin to say them to the Lord. Or sing to Him from your heart, a song that blesses His name. Don't sing to Him about your problems, or how your mother used to pray; but sing of His goodness, as the angels sang in Revelation 4:10, 11; 5:9-14; 7:11, 12.

Talk to Him, ask Him to forgive you; thank Him for His goodness, and for who He is. Thank Him for all that He has done for you. Build the altar (I Kings 18:32; Colossians 3:17)

Tell Him how great He is; how He has always kept His word.

Don't ask for anything - nothing - just love on Him.

Can't you feel His Spirit quicken you? This is God responding to your love!

Now, just sit quietly, and listen, as He speaks to your heart.

You are now building an altar to God.

Know that God wants us to minister to Him, to love on Him. His heart longs for this, just as we long for someone to love us.

The moment Jesus died on the cross, the veil between the Holy Place and the Holy of Holies in the temple was rent in two (Matthew 27:51).

This was done so that each of us, not just the priests, or the pastors, or the prophets could come before God to talk with Him, and spend time with Him. But that we too may come boldly before His throne!

Go, spend time with God! Minister to Him! He is waiting!

CHAPTER 5

Prophesying

I Corinthians 14:1-40

What does it mean to Prophesy? To speak what you hear God saying to you!
Ezekiel learns to prophesy.

Ezekiel 37:1-14

The hand of the Lord was upon me, and carried me out in the spirit of the Lord, and set me down in the midst of the valley which was full of bones.

And caused me to pass by them round about: and, behold, there were very many in the open valley; and, lo, they were very dry.

And he said unto me, Son of man, can these bones live? And I answered, O Lord God, thou knowest.

Again He said unto me, Prophesy upon these bones, and say unto them, O ye dry bones, hear the word of the Lord.

Thus saith the Lord God unto these bones; Behold, I will cause breath to enter into you, and ye shall live:

And I will lay sinews upon you, and will bring up flesh upon you, and cover you with skin, and put breath in you, and ye shall live; and ye shall know that I am the Lord.

So I prophesied as I was commanded: and as I prophesied, there was a noise, and behold a shaking, and the bones came together, bone to his bone.

And when I beheld, lo, the sinews and the flesh came up upon them, and the skin covered them above: but there was no breath in them.

Then said He unto me, Prophesy unto the wind, prophesy, son of man, and say to the wind, thus saith the Lord God; Come from the four winds, O breath, and breathe upon these slain, that they may live.

So I prophesied as He commanded me, and the breath came into them, and they lived, and stood up upon their feet, an exceeding great army.

Then He said unto me, Son of man, these bones are the whole house of Israel: behold, they say, Our bones are dried, and our hope is lost: we are cut off for our parts.

Therefore prophesy and say unto them, Thus saith the Lord God; Behold, O my people, I will open your graves, and cause you to come up out of your graves, and bring you into the land of Israel.

And ye shall know that I am the Lord, when I have opened your graves, O my people, and brought you up out of your graves.

And shall put my Spirit in you, and ye shall live, and I shall place you in your own land: then shall ye know that I the Lord have spoken it, and performed it, saith the Lord.

Who can prophesy? I want you to know that there is a difference between the office of a prophet and one who can prophesy.

God promised that all believers, filled with His Spirit would prophesy.

Joel 2:27-31

And ye shall know that I am in the midst of Israel, and that I am the Lord your God, and none else: and my people shall never be ashamed.

And it shall come to pass afterward, that I will pour out my Spirit upon all flesh; and your sons and your daughters shall prophesy, your old men shall dream dreams, your young men shall see visions:

And also upon the servants and upon the handmaids in those days will I pour out my Spirit.

And I will show wonders in the heavens and in the earth, blood, and fire, and pillars of smoke.

The sun shall be turned into darkness, and the moon into blood, before the great and the terrible day of the Lord come.

Peter confirms the prophesy of Joel on the day of Pentecost, when God's Spirit was poured out upon all flesh worshiping God in that room.

Acts 2:16-21

But this is that which was spoken by the prophet Joel;

And it shall come to pass in the last days, saith God, I will pour out of my Spirit upon all flesh: and your sons and your daughters shall prophesy, and your young men shall see visions, and your old men shall dream dreams.

And on my servants and on my handmaidens I will pour out in those days of my Spirit; and they shall prophesy:

And I will show wonders in heaven above, and signs in the earth beneath; blood, and fire, and vapor of smoke:

The sun shall be turned into darkness, and the moon into blood, before that great and notable day of the Lord come:

And it shall come to pass, that whosoever shall call on the name of the Lord shall be saved.

What is the Testimony of Jesus?

Revelation 19:9, 10

And he said unto me, Write, Blessed are they which are called unto the marriage supper of the Lamb. And he saith unto me, These are the true sayings of God.

And I fell at his feet to worship him. And he said unto me, See thou do it not: I am thy fellow servant, and of thy brethren that have the testimony of Jesus: worship God: for the testimony of Jesus is the Spirit of prophecy.

When was the Spirit of Prophecy operating in Jesus?

Every word that Jesus spoke was the very words He heard God say to Him. Some words were already written, such as when He was tempted in the wilderness, and He said, It is written. He did not have to ask God what to say, because He already knew. At other times, God was speaking directly to Jesus, and He would say what He heard God speaking to Him.

John 12:49, 50
For I have not spoken of myself; but the Father which sent me, He gave me a commandment, what I should say, and what I should speak.
And I know that His commandment is life everlasting: whatsoever I speak therefore, even as the Father said unto me, so I speak.

Sometimes God may not be speaking to your heart with His still small voice, but he may be giving you a visual picture: a vision, a dream, or a trance in which He will reveal a thing to you. In this visual picture God is telling you what to do or say.
Or it may be that as you were meditating or worshiping, the Lord brought to your remembrance a scripture in which Jesus did or said a certain thing. He is then instructing you to do or say that same thing.
Note: Some hear, some see, and some do both.

It was in 1997 that I learned about hearing the voice of God while attending a service in another city. There was a guest speaker who was teaching about prophesying. We were instructed to pray in the spirit, then ask God what He wanted to say to the person in front of us.
The instructor had told us that we may hear, or we may see, and some may do both. I partnered with a young woman, a stranger, to do the exercise with. It was agreed that I was to go first. After I prayed in tongues, I asked the Lord what He wanted to say to her. I had a vision in which I saw her standing before me, it was cloudy. There was a little girl, about five years old, standing on her right holding her hand. They were just standing. But I heard the Lord say, "Everything is going to be alright."
When I told the young woman what I saw and heard, she began to sob, saying aloud, Thank You Jesus! Thank You Jesus!
Because I did not know the young woman, to this day, I don't know what it was all about. But I do know that what I saw and heard was from God.

John 5:19-21
Then answered Jesus and said unto them, Verily, verily, I say unto you, The Son can do nothing of Himself, but what He seeth the Father do: for what things soever He doeth, these also doeth the Son likewise.

For the Father loveth the Son, and showeth Him all things that Himself doeth: and He will show Him greater works than these, that ye may marvel.

Throughout the book of Ezekiel, the prophet would hear God speaking, and he would then act out what ever God revealed to him. In doing so he was prophesying to the children of Israel.

Ezekiel 24:15-23
Also the word of the Lord came unto me, saying,
Son of man, behold, I take away from thee the desire of thine eyes with a stroke: yet neither shalt thou mourn nor weep, neither shall thy tears run down.
Forbear to cry, make no mourning for the dead, bind the tire of thine head upon thee, and put on thy shoes upon thy feet, and cover not thy lips, and eat not the bread of men.
So I spake unto the people in the morning, and at even my wife died; and I did in the morning as I was commanded.
And the people said unto me, Wilt thou not tell us what these things are to us, that thou doest so?
Then I answered them, The word of the Lord came unto me, saying,
Speak unto the house of Israel, Thus saith the Lord God; Behold, I will profane my sanctuary, the excellency of your strength, the desire of your eyes, and that which your soul pitieth; and your sons and your daughters whom ye have left shall fall by the sword.
And ye shall do as I have done: ye shall not cover your lips, nor eat the bread of men.
And your tires shall be upon your heads, and your shoes upon your feet: ye shall not mourn nor weep; but ye shall pine away for your iniquities, and mourn one toward another.

To prophesy is a spiritual gift. Paul teaches that we should desire to prophesy.

I Corinthians 14:1
Follow after charity, and desire spiritual gifts, but rather that ye may prophesy.

What most Christians don't realize is that you cannot perform a miracle unless God speaks it to you, (except the false prophets – Matthew 7:21-23).

Galatians 3:5
He therefore that ministereth to you in the Spirit, and worketh miracles among you, doeth he it by the works of the law, or by the hearing of faith?

The greatest miracle is salvation. Everyone who comes to Christ first hears God's voice calling them, even though they don't realize it. Because it is God who draws us, speaking to our hearts.
Most will tell you that "something" caused them to go forward to accept Jesus Christ as Lord and Savior. Jesus said Himself,

John 6:44

No man can come to me, except the Father which hath sent me **draw** him: and I will raise him up at the last day.

CHAPTER 6

How To Hear The Voice Of God

You will now learn how to hear the voice of God.

Matthew 16:13-19

When Jesus came into the coasts of Caesarea Philippi, He asked His disciples, saying, Whom do men say that I the Son of man am?

And they said, Some say that thou art John the Baptist: some, Elijah; and others, Jeremiah, or one of the prophets.

He saith unto them, But whom say ye that I am?

And Simon Peter answered and said, Thou art the Christ, the Son of the living God.

And Jesus answered and said unto him, **Blessed art thou, Simon Bar-jona: for flesh and blood hath not revealed it unto thee, but my Father which is in heaven.**

And I say also unto thee, That thou art Peter, and upon this rock I will build my church; and the gates of hell shall not prevail against it.

And I will give unto thee the keys of the kingdom of heaven: and whatsoever thou shalt bind on earth shall be bound in heaven: and whatsoever thou shalt loose on earth shall be loosed in heaven.

Jesus was telling Peter, You have learned to hear the voice of God!

Jesus is saying to us, You too **can hear** the voice of God!

I Corinthians 2:12

Now we have received, not the spirit of the world, but the spirit which is of God; that we might know the things that are freely given to us of God.

You, being a born again believer, filled with the Holy Ghost; have the Spirit of God within you. It is God's Spirit that speaks to us. Jesus said:

John 16:13-15

Howbeit when He, the Spirit of truth, is come, He will guide you into all truth: for He shall not speak of Himself: but whatsoever He shall hear, that shall He speak: and He will show you things to come.

He shall glorify me: for He shall receive of mine, and shall show it unto you.

All things that the Father hath are mine: therefore said I, that He shall take of mine, and shall show it unto you.

It is God's Holy Spirit who speaks to us.

It is a fact; God speaks to us everyday, in His still small voice.

The world calls it your conscience. But notice this fact, your conscience always tells you the right thing to do. This same voice will also convict you of sin.

The conscience is supposed to be your own thoughts. Now listen, you would not convict your self!

Notice I said, convict, not condemn. God does not condemn us. That is reserved unto Judgment day. Condemnation comes from another voice, the accuser, the devil, Satan.

Every day we hear God's voice speaking to us, telling us to go in this direction; or Don't eat too much of this; or Don't go back for seconds; or, Now, that was not nice for you to say; or, Say, Thank you; or Say, You're sorry; etc.

Let's learn how to hear the voice of God!

Exercise:

1.	Pray in the spirit; praying until you feel the quickening of your spirit.

2.	Stop praying.

3.	Speak aloud, saying, Jesus I love you.

4.	Be quiet and listen. Listen to His still small voice.

5.	What did He say to you? Was it, I love you too?

6.	You just heard the voice of God.

Talk to God everyday and listen to Him answer and talk to you. Become very familiar with His voice.

This is important; begin reading your Bible every day to be sure you are hearing God's voice and not the devil's. Sometimes the devil will say things that sound just like something God would say. The only way to know the difference is to read and meditate on the Word of God everyday. This way you will learn God's language, how He talks, and what He means when He says a thing.

Remember, the devil fooled Eve with God's word by twisting it ever so slightly. The devil fooled Peter too, in Matthew 16:21-23. He tried to fool Jesus, when Jesus was in the wilderness for forty days. Jesus passed the test because He knew the Word of God.

CHAPTER 7

How To Pray For Others

The Bible tells us we are to pray for one another. Here we will learn how to pray for those who come to us asking for prayer.

I Samuel 7:3-5

And Samuel spake unto all the children of Israel, saying, If ye do return unto the Lord with all your hearts, then put away the strange gods and Ashtaroth from among you, and prepare your hearts unto the Lord, and serve Him only: and He will deliver you out of the hand of the Philistines.

Then the children of Israel did put away Baalim and Ashtaroth, and served the Lord only.

And Samuel said, Gather all Israel to Mizpeh, and I will pray for you unto the Lord.

Matthew 19:13-15

Then were there brought unto Him little children, that He should put His hands on them, and pray: and the disciples rebuked them.

But Jesus said, Suffer little children, and forbid them not, to come unto me: for of such is the kingdom of heaven.

And He laid His hands on them, and departed thence.

We begin in the same manner that we learned to hear the voice of God. Praying within yourself; asking the Lord whether you are to touch the person you are about to pray for. If He says to touch them, then take their hands in yours. Do not hug them!

Exercise:

1.   Pray in the spirit (if you have them, pray in tongues), until your spirit is quickened.

2.   Stop.

3.   Ask the Lord what He would have you to pray for concerning the person in front of you, speaking the persons name.

4   Listen to His still small voice. And begin to speak what He is telling you to say. It may be very little that He gives you to speak. Or it may be very few words that you first hear, but begin to pray what you hear; more words may come. If not don't make up anything.

5.   End your prayer by thanking the Lord, and by speaking the words, "In the name of Jesus."

CHAPTER 8

How To Prophesy To Others

When we speak of prophesying we are not speaking of the office of a prophet. To prophesy means to be able to hear the voice of God, and speak what He says. God wants all of us to hear His voice. God wants all of us to speak His words.

I Corinthians 2:12, 13

Now we have received, not the spirit of the world, but the spirit which is of God; that we might know the things that are freely given to us of God.

Which things also we speak, not in the words which man's wisdom teacheth; but which the Holy Ghost teacheth; comparing spiritual things with spiritual.

Paul says that he would that all men prophesy.

I Corinthians 14:1-5

Follow after charity, and desire spiritual gifts, but rather that ye may prophesy.

For he that speaketh in an unknown tongue speaketh not unto men, but unto God: for no man understandeth him; howbeit in the spirit he speaketh mysteries.

But he that prophesieth speaketh unto men to edification, and exhortation, and comfort.

He that speaketh in an unknown tongue edifieth himself; but he that prophesieth edifieth the church.

I would that ye all spake with tongues, but rather that ye prophesied: for greater is he that prophesieth than he that speaketh with tongues, except he interpret, that the church may receive edifying.

Usually it is with the tongue of praise that one is edifying himself; which sounds quiet different that the tongues of prophesy. The tongues of prophesy quite often are spoken very boldly, with authority, because it is God speaking.

Peter is prophesying here (but not in tongues), using the very words of God that had been spoken by the prophet Joel.

Acts 2:16-18

But this is that which was spoken by the prophet Joel;

And it shall come to pass in the last days, saith God, I will pour out of my Spirit upon all flesh: and your sons and your daughters shall prophesy, and your young men shall see visions, and your old men shall dream dreams:

And on my servants and on my handmaidens I will pour out in those days of my Spirit:

and they shall prophesy:

When we prophesy we only prophesy in part. The prophecy that God gives to you may not make any sence to you, because it may not be for you. But what you hear you must speak. Only the person to whom it is to be given to will understand. They may share the meaning of it with you, or they may not. Do not fret over not knowing; trust in the Lord that you have spoken what He said to you.

I Corinthians 13:9
For we know in part, and we prophesy in part.

But in a service in which there will be prophesying, there should be someone present to record what is being said, either on paper, or on tape.

How to prophesy to others!

Exercise:

1. Pray in the Spirit.

2. Stop, be quiet.

3. Ask the Lord, "Father, What would You have me to say to ____ right now?

4. Listen to His still small voice. You may only see a vision, or you may only hear, or you may see and hear.

5. Tell the person what you heard and or saw.
Remember, it may not make any sence to you, but you must speak it.

CHAPTER 9

How To Receive A Word From God For Yourself

Did you know that you can receive a word from God for yourself!
It is true. David did this often to receive encouragement from God. That is why we have the book of Psalms.

Pull out a pencil and paper, and let's see how this is done!

Receiving a word for yourself

Exercise:

1.   Pray in the Spirit, aloud.

2.   Stop, be quiet.

3.   Ask the Lord, "Father, What would You like to say to me right now?

4.   Listen for His still small voice.

5.   Begin writing the first words that you hear. As you begin writing them, more will come. Don't concentrate on what you are writing, just write what you hear. Continue writing until He stops speaking.

6   Now, read to yourself the words you just wrote.

7.   You just received a word from the Lord.

CHAPTER 10

God Will Have You To Do And Say Things That Seem Foolish To The World

God will have you to do and say things that will seem foolish to the world.

I Corinthians 1:18-31

For the preaching of the cross is to them than perish foolishness; but unto us which are saved it is the power of God.

For it is written, I will destroy the wisdom of the wise, and will bring to nothing the understanding of the prudent.

Where is the wise? Where is the scribe? Where is the disputer of this world? Hath not God made foolish the wisdom of this world?

For after that in the wisdom of God the world by wisdom knew not God, it pleased God by the foolishness of preaching to save them that believe.

For the Jews require a sign, and the Greeks seek after wisdom:

But we preach Christ crucified, unto the Jews a stumblingblock, and unto the Greeks foolishness.

But unto them which are called, both Jews and Greeks, Christ the power of God, and the wisdom of God.

Because the foolishness of God is wiser than men; and the weakness of God is stronger than men.

For ye see your calling, brethren, how that not many wise men after the flesh, not many mighty, not many noble, are called:

But God hath chosen the foolish things of the world to confound the wise; and God hath chosen the weak things of the world to confound the things which are mighty;

And base things of the world, and things which are despised, hath God chosen, yea, and things which are not, to bring to naught things that are:

That no flesh should glory in His presence.

But of Him are ye in Christ Jesus, who of God is made unto us wisdom, and righteousness, and sanctification, and redemption:

That, according as it is written, He that glorieth, let him glory in the Lord.

What do we mean by this?

God may tell you to sacrifice your natural gift, which may be your trade.

By the world standards it was foolish for Jesus to leave a well paying career, to become a preacher without a steady income. So did the twelve disciples.

Paul gave up his wealth and the office of a Pharisee to preach the gospel (Galatians 1:11-14; Philippians 3:4-11).

God may tell you to separate yourself from your parents and siblings.

By the world standards, it was foolish for Jesus to ignore His mother and brethren, when they came to take Him, waiting outside the house, to save Him from the Pharisees (Matthew 10:34-39; 12:46-50).

By the world standards, it was foolish for God to tell Abraham to leave his father and his brothers, and go away, not knowing where he was going (Genesis 12:1-4).

God may tell you to go to a church, and speak a word that will anger the congregation and the pastor.

By the world standards, It was foolish for Jesus, just beginning His ministry, on the Sabbath, to go into the synagogue and upset the rules when He said, Ye will surely say unto me this proverb, Physician, heal thyself. And He said, No prophet is accepted in His own country (Luke 4:16-29).

There were plots to kill Jeremiah, he was also put on trial, and thrown into prison many times for speaking what God told him to speak. And many other prophets were killed for doing the same (Jeremiah 26:1-24).

God may tell you to leave your church, listen to His voice, and go where ever He says to go, and stay as long as He tells you to stay.

Abraham, Isaac, and Jacob were directed by God as to where to go and how long to stay.

Peter was led by the Spirit of God to go to certain cities to preach the word. So were Philip, Paul, and Barnabas.

You will not be church hopping; as some call it, but if you will be observant, God will be teaching you from each experience.

Are you bold enough to step out in faith when you hear God directing you? Are you bold enough to say and do anything God tells you to say and do?

(MY TESTIMONY, CONTINUED FROM THE INTRODUCTION):

For about a month I tried to sell my business, but could not. Then one Friday morning, while I was on my way to work, the Lord spoke to me and said, Today is your last day here, go through the shop and take out everything you want.

That morning I went through the shop and only brought out a hand full of things. There was by estimate, about thirty thousand dollars in merchandise in that place. But I wanted none of it (later in December, I auctioned everything off.)

I closed the shop that Friday evening, never to return. On Sunday morning, following service I rededicated my life to the Lord, and announced the closing of my shop, to the church. They all thought that I was crazy.

On Monday afternoon, while my husband was at his garage, and my children were in school, I was sitting on the couch in my living room reading my Bible. I took a rest and the Lord spoke to me, saying, Do you know what you said on yesterday? I answered, Yes, I know what I said (sarcastically), I said, I rededicate my life to the Lord. He said, Say it again. And I said, I re.....

That is as far as I got with my sentence. I had been sitting on the couch one minute, saying these words; the next minute, I found myself standing with both hands raised up, praising the Lord, and saying, Lord I'll do whatever You want me to do!

He spoke to me again, saying, When you ran your business, you didn't just rent the tuxedos, you didn't just bake the wedding cakes, and you didn't just do the flowers for the wedding. Everything that the bride needed to prepare herself for her wedding, you did for her. And I want you to do the same for me.

The only thing I could say was, Yes, Lord!

So I accepted my call by God into the ministry, even though I had been taught that women are not supposed to preach. By the next Sunday, I was making the announcement to the church about my call. Little did I realize that it would be here, in the church, that I would face my greatest persecution. For these Disciples of Christ didn't believe in women ministers either. By then we had gotten a new pastor, a young man, eight years younger than I. Actually, he was still a young convert to the gospel. He had gotten saved one year, called into the ministry the following year, and he was pastoring our church the next year, (what Paul calls a novice). By him being a novice, there was much contention between the two of us.

I tried to be obedient to my pastor, but the Lord would always tell me to do the opposite of what the pastor said to do. By 1997, I was experiencing much persecution in the church that I was attending, because I believed God's every word. I believed not just His written word, but I knew when God was speaking to me. It was not an audible voice, but He spoke to my heart with His still small voice; and He would confirm it to me through His written word.

I had learned that we all should have the gift of tongues, and I wanted them. If the disciples spoke in tongues, then I wanted to speak in tongues. I sought the Lord hard for this gift, doing much fasting and praying. And then one night while attending a prayer meeting in a little mobile home, the gift of tongues came. I was so excited.

But then one Saturday morning the pastor had a meeting with two other ministers from the church, and me. He commanded us that we were not to lay hands on anyone, we were not to use the oil, and we were not to speak in tongues in his church. My heart was grieved, and so was God's heart. And I cried.

In September of that year, I had been invited to a Women's Conference at a church in Greensboro, NC. During one of the sessions, one of the speakers had told us that we should obey our pastor at all times. But she also said that we should obey God. And this confused me. So I went to her after she had finished speaking, and told her about my dilemma. She asked me why I was still at that church. I told her that God had not told me to leave yet. She asked me again, and I said, My husband is not going to leave.

When I said this she said, I'm not the person that you should be talking to, I am not married. And she called one of the other female evangelists over to talk with me. She first told her about my dilemma. This woman said to me, Let's pray. We held hands, and she prayed in tongues. Then she told me that God would take me out of that church, but I had to wait. I had to wait on my husband, even if it took five days or five years.

Later, during this conference, the main speaker called all the women who had been called into the ministry to come forward, so that she could pray for each of us. When she got to me, she held out her right hand towards me and prayed silently. Then she said to me, God said, Don't be afraid.

Afraid of what, I had not idea. But I knew it was God.

The next morning I was preparing to attend church, when I got a phone call from the other female minister in our church. She said that God had told her that I had a word for her. I told her that I didn't know what it was. But I then told her about the service I had attended on Saturday, and about a dream that I'd had that Saturday before going to the conference.

In the dream, I was in the house in which I grew up in, I had gotten up before daylight to get ready to go on an outing. I was in the kitchen making a turkey sandwich when I looked out of the window, and saw a limousine pull up in front of the house. After the car stopped a man wearing a top hat and tails, got out to open the car door. Someone got out and came into the house. It was my aunt. She said to me, Puddin, we are ready to go.

I told her that they would have to wait, because I was making me a turkey sandwich. She said, But we don't have time. I said, Tell them to wait.

But when she went back to the limousine, she got in and the car pulled off without me. I decided to make a second turkey sandwich. And I said, I'll just catch up with them at the next stop. I finished packing my sandwiches and turned to go into the hallway to get my shoes and go. There the dream ended.

I told the minister that God had given me the interpretation of the dream, after I had returned from the conference, and had called a woman who had told me that she would go with me to the conference, but did not go. When I called the woman, she was not home, and her daughter told me that her mother had gone with the women of our church to Greensboro, to bowl.

The Lord said to me, The limo represented the church today, and those inside the limo represented those who hold on to the world instead of seeking Him. The turkey sandwich represented the meat of the word. Two turkey sandwiches meant a double portion. The Lord told me that I had received a double portion, because I was seeking to know Him, instead of going bowling.

When I told the minister on the phone this, she then began to scream in my ear, praising the Lord. Then she gave me a word. She said to me, You had better say what ever God is telling you to say! When she said these words the Spirit of the Lord came upon me, and I too, began to shout, praising the Lord. So much so, that my husband came running into the living room to see what was the matter. But I could say nothing, just continue to praise the Lord.

I got dressed, as I was instructed by the Lord, to wear my red dress, with white accessories. He said, The red is for the blood of Jesus, and the white is for the purity under the blood. I knew something was about to happen, but what, I did not know.

The pastor had asked the male minister to be master of ceremony that morning. That meant that he was the master of ceremony. He told me to lead in reading the affirmation of faith during the service.

The other minister had not gotten to church as yet, but when she did, that is when the ball began to roll. She opened the door to the pastor's study, and spoke to him first, then to the other minister, who was sitting just inside the door. To speak to me, she would have to open the door wider just to see me. She did. And when she did, she gasped.

I had been looking down, but when I heard her catch her breath, I looked up to see what the matter was. She was looking at me with her mouth wide open. And then I saw it, we were both dressed alike; in red and white.

She told me that hers was a summer suit, and she had put it away for the winter. But the Lord had told her to take it back out and wear it to church that morning. My heart began to flutter.

The master of ceremony told her what he wanted her to do. She was to read James 3:1-12. She opened her Bible to read before going into the sanctuary. And again she gasped. We were sitting beside one another. So I looked at her Bible to see what she was reading. And again my heart began to flutter. I knew then what God wanted me to do. The heading in my Bible for James 3, said 'The Tongue.' I knew that I was to speak in tongues that morning, after we had gone into the pulpit.

I was still new at this, and did not know how to turn the tongues on whenever I wanted to. So I told the Lord that He would have to help me with this.

When we got into the pulpit, the congregation was almost finished with what they called testimony service. One of the deacons was giving a testimony. One minute he was serious, the next he was telling a joke.

The Lord spoke to me and said, You are drinking the vinegar. I understood: when Jesus was on the cross, they brought Him vinegar to dull the pain and prolong the agony. But He refused to drink of it.

About that time the deacon sat down, and the others stood to close out that part of the service. But they could not because I had stood. I did not know what to do, so I said, No one knows what I have been through but me and the Lord.

By the time I had finished saying these words, both my hands were raised, and I felt the urge to bend forward to bow. I did. Then with my hands still stretched out, I began to raise up, and that is when the tongues began to roll from my belly, out of my mouth. I stood there speaking in tongues for a good few minutes. At the same time, saying within myself, Lord God, please give us the interpretation! I knew that I was not speaking in a tongue of praise, but a prophetic utterance.

It was so quiet in that church, except for my voice; you could hear a pin drop on that red carpet. But as soon as I stopped speaking, the other female minister began to give the interpretation: while walking around the pulpit seven times. The Lord had me to count the number of times she walked around it.

She also gave a prophetic word to the head deacon. The week before he had fallen off of his tractor, and it had almost run over him, but "something" had stopped it. She told him that it had been God who stopped it.

The master of ceremony took over then and closed that part of the service out. The pastor came forward and said, This was God, and I have never seen Him manifest Himself this way. But it was done decent and in order, and there is no need for anyone to say anything. He then went on to preach from James 3:1-12.

I remember the pastor saying in his message; You can't get sweet water and bitter water out of the same fountain. But other than that I don't remember what he said. I was so excited, because of the way that God had manifested Himself at the beginning of the service. I knew with all my heart that there would be some changes about to happen in our church, for the better, and God would be in charge instead of man.

How little did I understand that God was setting me up for my departure.
As soon as the pastor had greeted the last person at the door of the church, as they left, he came to the other female minister and I, and told us to come to his study. We both followed him, expecting exciting news. But what followed completely floored me.

When we walked into the pastor's study, the room was filled with the deacons of the church and the other male minister; or I should say, it was filled with the Sanhedrin council. And the other minister and I were about to be put on trial. The pastor began with this question; Was this the two of you doing this, or was this God?

I was so stunned at his question, that I could not say a word. The other minister asked him to repeat the question. And he asked, Did the two of you set this up? We both just shook our heads, answering, no. There were more questions, but I was too shocked to open my mouth to answer, so I just shook my head to respond with a yes or no. To think that God had manifested Himself to the whole congregation, and even the pastor had not recognized Him! The master of ceremony had said that he didn't believe the interpretation that the other female minister had given. He said, Because in her interpretation, God had said that there was no love in that church.

At the end of our trial, we were told to leave everything alone, not to do anything. The elder even said, We all must let it go; if the two of them are doing this, then nothing will come of it. But if it is God, we cannot stop it. And the meeting was dismissed.

For several days I was in shock, because of what had happened. Then I went to God, asking questions. He told me to read the book of Luke, the fourth chapter. This is when Jesus returns from the wilderness, goes to His own home church, and preaches His initial sermon. When He finishes, they force Him out of the building, and try to cast Him over the brow of the hill, to kill Him.

The Lord also led me to the book of Acts, when the disciples came before the Sanhedrin council. There, the very words that the head deacon had spoken in the meeting we had attended, the Pharisee, Gamaliel had spoken to the council and to the high priest (Acts 5:38, 39). I had not been thrown out; therefore I knew it was not over.

Then on Friday evening, the pastor called me. He said he wanted to ask me a question. The question was, Would you be willing to take a class? I asked him, What kind of class. He said, It is called, The Divine Order Of The Gift You Have. I then asked, What is it about? He said, It is about the gift of tongues that you have, and the gift of interpretation that the other sister has. I asked, Who would be attending the class? And he said, Just the three of us. And we won't even meet at the church.

I told him that it sounded interesting. Then I asked, Who is teaching it? He said, I am. I said, No, I will not take it. He got very upset and tried to preach to me about the importance of me being obedient to him. He even said to me, Since you were called into the ministry, the devil has been trying to steal your ministry. And now you are going to let him take it!

But how could he teach us about the gift of tongues, when he had already told us not to do it in his church.

I opened my mouth (at the time I did not know where the words came from), and I said, God called me, and gave me this ministry, and can't no demon in hell take it away from me!

He then got very upset. He then told me good by. I hung up the phone, and began to talk with God. Had I done the wrong thing? And God said, No!

The pastor called the other female minister to talk with her. When they had finished their conversation, he told her to call me, and have me to call him; because it was too late for him to be calling a woman. It was after 11pm.

By this time my husband, who was working second shift at the time, had come home from work. I told him what had happened. He asked me, Who else is coming to the class? I told him what the pastor had said to me: that it would only be the three of us. Not even the other male minister would know about it.

My husband said, No, you are not going to any classes with that man.

It was after my husband had come in that I returned the pastors call. He listened while I talked with the pastor; asking again who would be attending, and would the deacons be there? The pastor said, No, no one but the three of us will be attending. And again I told him, No. He said, Good by. I thought that was the end of it.

Again I was wrong. The very next morning, the pastor called me to ask me to come to a meeting that evening at 5pm. I told him I would be there. He called a second time, asking if my husband could come too. I asked my husband, he told me he was supposed to work, but he would go with me to the meeting.

That evening we went to church. Someone met us and told us that we were meeting in the fellowship hall, which is a separate building behind the church. I thought that this was strange, but we walked to the rear of the church building to the fellowship hall.

The pastor was holding a secret council meeting without informing all of the board members. Later the Lord reminded me that they had done the same thing to Jesus before they crucified Him.

Seated inside were several of the deacons, the male minister, and the secretary of the church (who was very devoted to the pastor), along with the pastor. Two of the deacons were on the board of the church. The others, I knew, would agree with whatever the pastor said, even the secretary. None of them knew what the meeting was all about.

He opened the meeting with prayer, and then he informed them that the Lord had given him a word earlier that day. He said the Lord had given to him the scripture about Moses and Aaron, and their disobedience when they struck the rock instead of simply speaking to it.

He told them that I was Moses, in this case, and the other female minister (who had not been informed about the meeting), was Aaron. He said that as Moses and Aaron had been disobedient to God, we had been disobedient to him. He told them that he had planned to teach a class called The Divine Order Of The Gift That You Have. He said he was going to teach it to all the deacons, and the ministers.

He told them that one of the female ministers had agreed to take the class, and the other had refused. He told them that I was the one who had refused. And because I had refused to obey the pastor, he was sitting me down from the pulpit. And He needed the board to come into agreement with him.

The men were a little taken back. I had been at that church for twenty years, and everything they had ever asked me to do, I had done. But because he was the pastor, they all agreed with him.

I then asked if I could speak, and he said, Yes. But before I could get three words out of my mouth, he slammed his hands down on the table and said, Let's dismiss. He then closed out the board meeting with what he called a prayer, and dismissed.

My husband, Lawrence and I were about to go home, when they informed us that church conference was about to start in the church sanctuary. They told us that we needed to be there. So we went.

When we walked into the sanctuary, the elder deacon asked for someone to lead a song. He asked one of the deacons to read a scripture. And he asked the male minister to pray. Then something strange happened. The deacon picked up an old Bible from behind the pew, and some of the pages fell out. He picked them up from the floor and stuck them back in the Bible.

One of the men, who had been in the board meeting in the fellowship hall, began to sing a song. This was very unusual, because, even during church service, this man never sang. On top of that, the song that he sang was the same song that I had been singing at home all week. The name of the song is "Tis So Sweet To Trust In Jesus."

When I heard this and noticing who had started singing the song, I knew God was about to manifest Himself.

Next the deacon got up to read the scripture. Again the pages fell out of the old Bible. He picked them up, and stuck them back in the Bible, making a joke about Corinthians being in the book of Genesis. He then just opened the Bible, and the first place his eyes fell on, he began to read aloud. By the time he had finished the third verse, I knew the Lord was speaking to me through the scriptures.

The deacon was reading John 16:1-4. When he got to the fourth verse he paused, because he realized what he was saying; although no one else in the room was listening but my husband and me.

He had not looked for a scripture to read, but the Lord had caused him to turn to it and read. It was then that my husband's knee hit mine. And I said to the Lord, Lord, I hear You, but what must I do. And he said, Just listen.

The deacon began to read again. In the scripture, Jesus was saying to His disciples, I must go away. And I understood that the Lord was telling me, it is time for me to leave this church. So I wrote a note to my husband, saying, When this meeting is over, I have to leave this church. Are you going with me?

After he read the note, he turned to me and spoke aloud, saying, Yes!

We could not leave just yet. The pastor had to make the announcement to the church, informing them of the fact that he was sitting me down from the pulpit. After he had made the announcement, I asked if I could say something. The elder deacon was in charge. He said I could speak.

I stood and said, God called me to be a minister in this church. But if I cannot do what God has called me to do here, then I must leave.

I then turned to the members behind me, and told them that I loved them. And if they ever needed me, they knew where I lived, and they knew my phone number. And my husband and I walked out of that church that night; to begin a new adventure.

It was after we left the church that I found that I had more time on my hands. There were no more weekly meetings to attend, so I spent my time reading and studying the Bible.

While studying, during that time, the Lord revealed to me the teaching which I call Foundational Truths Hebrews 5:12; 6:1, 2. I began to write it down, and soon found that I had a book. I also had the opportunity to attend other churches, and teach it to them.

Between 1997, when we left the church, and 1999, Lawrence, our children, and I had attended several churches, but could not seem to fit in. Two of the churches we actually joined and left. We stayed in one about six months, in the other nine months. Then Lawrence came home from work one day and told me that I had a new nick name, "PCH." When I asked him what this meant, he said, Professional Church Hoppers!

Then in October 1999, the Lord told me that it was time to begin my ministry. He had given me a name for the ministry the day after I was set down from the pulpit. The name of the ministry is New Commandment Ministries.

I was hesitant at first, not knowing what to do. But after He had spoken to me several times to get started, I knew that I had to be obedient. So, Lawrence, our children, and I began having service in our home on Sunday. And just as the Lord guided me in my bridal business, He has also guided me every step of the way in my ministry.

New Commandment Ministries is very different from the main line churches. We don't have church. On Sundays we have what most would call a prayer meeting, which has no program. We are strictly led by the Lord.

During the week I teach Foundational Truths to the new comers; which usually last about five to six months. Those who come are informed that they are only here for a season. They are here to learn, and then go out and practice what they have learned.

In July 2005, the Lord informed me that I did not have the whole teaching. He then gave to me what I thought was the complete lesson. This second teaching is to be separate from the other, He said. The name of it is called "The Ten Commandments, The Foundation Of The Kingdom Of God." When I finished it, He told me to have it published.

But as soon as I had finished writing the last page, the Lord informed me that there is more. He said to me, First, people need to know that they can hear My voice. He gave to me the words for this teaching also. And there you have this book from which you are reading, "Hearing The Voice Of God, The Foundation Of The Church." He always gives me everything backward, beginning with the end.

You have just finished reading my testimony. I write this to you not to condemn anyone, but to reveal to you that in order to have a testimony; you must experience the same things that Jesus experienced. To have a testimony you must first have heard the voice of God for yourself, and obeyed Him, and not man.

Everything that I have experienced since the moment that God called me into the ministry was because God was directing me; just as it was the Spirit of God that led Jesus into the wilderness.

Think about it, for a person to walk off into the wilderness and stay for forty days without food, is strange. So why did Jesus do it? Why? Because God told Him to do it. He had to be proved, tested, and tried by the fire!

If you too have been called into the ministry, and you are experiencing much persecution, know that this work is being done because God is directing it. He is in charge. Will you obey Him, or will you conform to the world's way of thinking? Listen to the still small voice of the Holy Spirit, and obey God. Read your Bible every day that you might receive understanding.

Get to know God's word! Get the wisdom of God; get the understanding of His wisdom; come to understand what He means when He speaks; get to know the difference between God's voice and the devil's voice. The devil speaks to you too, ask Peter (Matthew 16:21-23).

The only way you can know the difference between God's voice and the devil's voice is to have a daily personal relationship with God. The only way a bank teller knows the difference between a real dollar bill and a fake one is to become very familiar with the real dollar bill.

I want you to note another thing. Every minister's ministry is different. The only way that you will know exactly what God wants you to do is to listen to His voice, obey, and stay in the Word. Read it daily! Read it daily! Read it daily!

When John the Baptist began his ministry, it was something new, he was the first to baptize with water. When Jesus began His ministry, it was something new, He was the first to baptize with the Holy Ghost and with fire! When Paul began his ministry, his too was something new, he was the first to teach the Gentiles. Each of their ministries were diverse from the other, yet they all had one thing in common: they all heard the voice of God and obeyed.

It is not enough to read through and study the lesson that you have just completed, you must put it into practice.

Jesus said, God's house is a house of prayer!

So the services at New Commandment Ministries are based on that fact. We have no rituals, no programs, and no itinerary. Our services are centered on prayer, teaching people how to pray, teaching them how to hear the voice of God, and teaching them obedience to God.

Our services are not what one might call a formal church service, nor are they traditional nor contemporary. They are more like a prayer meeting, and informal.

Although we do worship, pray, and preach during the service, we also have healing, prophesying and interpretation. But from week to week one never knows what order things may happen.

Jesus ran the money changers out of the temple; therefore we have no soliciting or selling of merchandise. The offering box is set up in the room so that people can place their tithes and offerings in the box at any time, without interrupting service. This is the same way it was done in the temple, in the Old Testament and in the New Testament.

It is a joy serving the Lord in this capacity, for it allows me to see the different gifts that operate in people who attend here, and it allows me to help bring that gift forward. And, at the same time not be jealous of their gifts.

In them realizing their gift they develop a deeper relationship with God and His Son

Jesus Christ. And I thank the Lord for giving me this opportunity!

I do pray that you learn to pray - communicate with God, and develop such a closeness with Him, that will endure until the coming of Christ Jesus! I pray that after reading through the three teachings, that you will have a better understanding of God's word as you read it. I pray that you will be able to see Christ Jesus more clearly.

Please do not take these books as the Gospel, but as an aid to the Gospel of Jesus Christ.

Other books by Cassandra Broadnax

Hearing The Voice Of God, The Foundation Of The Church

The Ten Commandments, The Foundation Of The Kingdom Of God

Foundational Truths, Hebrews 5:12; 6:1, 2

Introduction To Ministry, The Three Visions

To Contact:

Cassandra Broadnax
New Commandment Ministries, Inc.

Email: ncommmin@aol.com

www.ingramcontent.com/pod-product-compliance
Lightning Source LLC
Chambersburg PA
CBHW081226020426
42331CB00012B/3095